Adam + Lisa,

During times ~~_____~~ly,
it helps to face fear with facts.
Our Company is making these
books available to do just
that.   Hope you guys are

Safe + Well!

Michael + Kimberlie Hess
720-253-6174

HOW MONEY WORKS

Stop being a
SUCKER

Tom Mathews | **Steve Siebold**

HOW**MONEY**WORKS

howmoneyworks.com

Special thanks to:

Jane Evans, Jeff Gaines, Matt Luckey, Brian Maddox, Angie McCart, J.D. Phillips, Kim Scouller, and Dawn Siebold.

For more information: licensing@howmoneyworks.com
Creative direction, design, and production by Outstand®
Essentials Edition, October 2019

HAMMERHEADS™
PUBLISHING

To anyone who has ever felt like a sucker because
someone else knew more about money:

This book is for you.

Featuring the cast of How**Money**Works®

Stop being a sucker? Well that's offensive.

Sarah - 49, Real Estate Agent

Some may forget to dot their i's and cross their t's, but not Sarah. Especially not in the word "stickler." While not known for tact, Sarah's honesty and persistence have helped her remain a top producer for over a decade.

Mei - 56, History Professor

Mei's students all share two fond memories from her class. Her favorite expression: "It's possible to be both nice and precise." And "Jeopardy Day", when the students get to be contestants and Mei gets to be Alex Trebek.

The definition of a sucker is "one who is easily fooled."

Sounds like us!

TJ - 32, Medical Sales

TJ was made for sales and sales were made for TJ. He's got the only infectious things any doctor would ever want in their office—a deadly smile and a killer personality.

They're just trying to get our attention, guys.

Well, I reckon they got it.

Dana - 42, Hospital Director

Smart and energetic, Dana is the kind of high-performing executive everyone wants to be in the room with. Everyone except those who aren't doing their jobs. Why? Because they all know Dana doesn't play.

George - 67, Retired Military Officer

Civilian life suits George well. Aside from restoring the old Mustang, he Facebooks with friends, FaceTimes with family, and facepalms over today's teens, who could all benefit from a butt-kicking bootcamp... in his opinion.

I don't know about
you all, but I'm no sucker.

Dude, you're literally
sucking on a sucker.

Clark - 36, Ride Share Driver

He has a "brilliant" idea for an app if he could just raise enough cash... from anyone who wants in on the dream. Until then, it's the ride share thing. Flexible hours. No cubicles. Captive audience. What's not to love?

Zoey - 19, University Student

Zoey can't decide between physical therapy or marine biology. The choice would be simpler if people were as appreciative as animals when you do something nice for them. And by "people" she means her roommates.

We've all got lots to
learn. LET'S DO THIS!

Hector - 28, Restaurant Owner

A born motivator, Hector runs a small fleet of food trucks. Social media made his sandwiches a city-wide success, which is why he named the business, "Social Sandwich."

Contents

Introduction

I never read intros.

Why not? This one seems short and
sweet and to the point—like me.

66

An investment in knowledge
pays the best interest.

– BENJAMIN FRANKLIN

Who can argue with
that? I'll give it a shot.

Master chefs become obsessed with how food works. Coaches study how winning teams work. Golfers watch and rewatch how pro swings work. Generals dissect how the battles of conquerors work. You get the idea.

Money is no different. Those who study how money works have a greater chance of becoming wealthy. As they learn, they stop doing stupid things, start measuring their decisions, and begin leveraging information to make smarter moves. Knowledge corrects behavior. Correct behavior alters the future.

There's an old saying: "What we think about, we bring about." The expression holds true over the course of our lives in determining both our struggles and our successes. What you think about becomes your reality.

What will your reality be?

It will largely depend on how you think about money.

If you're like many, you think primarily in emotional terms. You get excited to buy something new. You grow frustrated when paying bills. Because you find the mechanics of money uninteresting and confusing, you end up like so many others—never learning how money really works.

No big deal, right? But here's the thing about money. It's not like cooking, golfing, or any other skill you can get by without. If you don't know how to properly grill salmon, who cares? If you can't drain a 20-foot putt, so what? But if you don't know how money works, you might wake up every day wondering why life SUCKS.

That's a strong word, but yes, not knowing how money works... sucks.

It sucks up your time. It sucks up your freedom. And, most importantly, it sucks up your income. So where does it all go? It goes to your mortgage lender, your credit card company, your bank, Apple, Amazon, Netflix. You know—the guys who know exactly how money works. W.C. Fields said, "It's morally wrong to allow a sucker to keep his money."

This is what you're up against.

You become a sucker. They become wealthy.

The world is full of people who are happy to tell you what to do with your money.

This book is designed to help you learn how money really works so you can stop being a sucker, start being a student, and be the one to call the shots throughout your life with confidence.

Grand failure or grand finale?

You choose. It all starts with your thinking. It all starts with knowing how money works.

So how about now, TJ? Ready to learn how money works?

Mei... you were right.

Told ya.

1 | REALITIES

Financial Illiteracy is the #1 Economic Crisis in the World

Financial literacy is knowing how money works. Or, as the Federal Reserve Bank of St. Louis states: "It means understanding how to earn, spend, save, manage and invest money... Having a strong understanding of financial literacy will allow you to make better financial decisions that can hopefully improve your day-to-day life."[1]

Financial illiteracy, on the other hand, is NOT knowing how money works, which can make you financially unwell... for life.

Come on, the #1 economic crisis in the world?

Skeptical, George? Have you considered that financial literacy is the one economic factor that can directly affect all 7.5 billion people in the world?

No, I hadn't. That's a pretty big deal.

Financial illiteracy plagues people all over the world, in every country.

Currently, 90% of Venezuelans live below the poverty line. Greece still hovers close to 20% unemployment since their 2010 economic collapse. These are just two examples of nations suffering from an economic state of emergency.

The reasons for each crisis differ, including fallout from the global recession, military turmoil, political corruption, natural disasters, and a wide range of other causes and complexities. The deep anguish millions of people endure every day due to economic disasters should never be diminished. However, the number of people affected by the troubles of national economies pales in comparison to the widespread crisis of financial illiteracy.

Financial illiteracy impacts almost three-fourths of the world.

Financial illiteracy is the lack of education about money and finance—especially personal finance. It enables governments and corporations, driven to meet the demands of stakeholders and shareholders, to leverage the ignorance of citizens and customers for their own power and gain.

Throughout the world, it is chiefly knowledge that separates those with advantages from those who are taken advantage of.

The goal of this book is to close that gap by democratizing education about how money works. When everyone is financially literate, the playing field can be leveled, giving citizens from each nation the chance to enjoy a higher quality of life and the hope to pursue their dreams for the future.

A recent study on financial literacy found that only 30% of people in the world are financially literate.[2]

There are over 7.5 billion people in the world. That means over 5 billion people are financially illiterate.

Now you see why it's the #1 economic crisis in the world, Mei.

Indisputably. The sheer size of the problem is staggering.

Financial illiteracy is the #1 economic crisis in America too.

If you think America is leading in financial literacy, you're wrong. A recent study reveals that Americans trail behind Germany, Canada, France, India, and Spain in financial literacy.[2]

Take a look at these facts[3] that reveal the damage financial illiteracy has caused in America:

 44% of Americans don't have enough cash to cover a $400 emergency.

 43% of student loan borrowers are not making payments.

 38% of households in America have credit card debt.

 33% of American adults have zero retirement savings.

Ugh. You know, those numbers are just hard to even process.

In a recent survey, U.S. adults said that, on average, they lost $1,230 dollars in 2018 because they didn't properly understand basic household finance issues.

And almost 20% lost $2,500.[4]

– THE NATIONAL FINANCIAL EDUCATORS COUNCIL

This explains a lot. Being a real estate agent, I talk to people every day who struggle to afford the home they really want. If these numbers are true, many are squandering an entire mortgage payment.

Altogether, Sarah, the lack of financial literacy cost Americans a total of $295 billion in 2018.[4]

I don't mean to be rude, but do people even want financial literacy?

They do, Sarah. It's just not available.

In another recent survey, American young adults were asked what high school-level course would benefit them the most. The majority answered, "Money Management (Personal Finance)."[5]

I thought this stuff was taught in schools. It has to be. I'd bet $50 on it.

I'll take that bet!

66

Only 17 out of 50 states require
high schools to teach at least
one class in personal finance.[6]

– COUNCIL FOR ECONOMIC EDUCATION

Yeah, and mine wasn't
one of them.

Man, I guess I really am a sucker.
I just got played by a 19-year-old.

A strong case can be made that financial literacy is the most neglected core life skill.

Why isn't personal finance taught in schools?

Public schools around the country are receiving funding for S.T.E.M. and S.T.E.A.M. programs on mobile game design, dance choreography, and even hydroponic farming, all requiring expensive equipment, studios, and labs. It should prompt everyone to ask why the education system can't fund a Personal Finance 101 course.

If the reasoning isn't lack of funding, what's the rationale?

Kinda makes you wonder...

If it's by design or just the way it is, without the knowledge of how money works, people get stuck.

The lack of financial literacy doesn't just make people suckers, it traps them in the Sucker Cycle—often for life.

Hey, watch who you're callin' a sucker! The average American doesn't make a whole heckuva lot. It's no wonder they feel trapped.

Instead of putting their money to work, the sucker spends his or her money foolishly or deposits it into a low interest account. Why? Instant gratification and ignorance. They simply don't know what else to do with it. Essentially, the sucker gets a paycheck from someone wealthy, then hands their money back to someone else wealthy, who then makes more money with the sucker's money.

Paycheck

the Sucker Cycle

Low Interest Rate Savings Account

No one has money.

For each generation, it's the same. The knowledge of how money works is not taught from K-12. High school graduates head off to universities. They don't learn about personal finance there either. College graduates enter the work force and start receiving a paycheck... and spending their paycheck.

And the Sucker Cycle continues. Earn a paycheck. Spend a paycheck. Earn a paycheck. Spend a paycheck.

They join the hundreds of millions living paycheck-to-paycheck. Always spending. Barely saving. When retirement finally arrives or when accidents or illnesses occur later in life, a terrible realization comes over them...

They have no money.

According to a recent survey:[7]

- Millennials have saved a median amount of $23,000 for retirement
- Gen-Xers have saved a median amount of $66,000 for retirement
- Baby Boomers have saved a median amount of $152,000 for retirement
- 7 in 10 Baby Boomers plan to continue working after age 65

So, what yer say'n is that everyone has money, but almost no one has money... saved.

You nailed it, George.

Most Americans make enough to put their money to work. They just don't understand enough beyond earning and spending. Numbers don't lie.

How much can you save? If you've ever asked yourself that question, the answer is you could save $378 each month by cutting these non-necessities in half.

Monthly spending habits by the typical American:[8]

 Eat Out & Take Out
$181/mo.

 Coffee & Lattes
$60/mo.

 Ride Shares
$83/mo.

 Alcohol
$29/mo.

 Events
$30/mo.

 New Clothing
$63/mo.

 Lottery Tickets
$74/mo.

 Subscription Services
$237/mo.

P.T. Barnum once said, "There's a sucker born every day."

It was "every minute," but who's counting...

How the sucker thinks.

"The haves and have-nots. It's the way things have always been and I guess it's the way things will always be."

How the wealthy think.

"I may not have learned about personal finance in school, but with the right information, the economic crisis of financial illiteracy doesn't have to be my personal crisis."

What have you learned?

The economic crisis of financial illiteracy affects the entire _____.

The crisis is so widespread because financial literacy is largely not taught in _____.

People get stuck in a cycle of foolish _____ and putting money in low interest _____ accounts.

Mei: world
George: schools
Sarah: spending, savings

2 | REALITIES

You're a Sucker

For bragging rights,
guess the number of jelly beans in the jar.

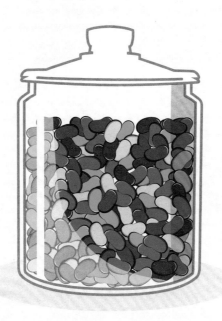

A lot!

Guess accepted.

Wait! That wasn't my guess...

Would anyone else
like to guess?

I guess 2,100
jelly beans.

955

1,450

Guesses accepted.
Anyone else?

What's the volume of
the jar in liters?

Smart question.
It's 2 liters.

Thank you. I guess
490 jelly beans.

Dana wins! The answer is 500 jelly beans!

Dana, how did
you know?

While you guys were
guessing, I googled how
many jelly beans fit
in a liter. It's 245.
So, I doubled it.

Wow. I thought it'd
be a whole lot more.

We weren't told we
could google it...

We weren't told we couldn't.

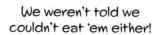

Clark... what ARE
you doing?

We weren't told we
couldn't eat 'em either!

Most people don't know beans about money.

In 2018, a global survey asked over 100,000 people in 15 different countries 3 simple questions about money concepts. 70% failed to answer all three basic questions correctly.[2]

No future should be left to a wild guess.

The Jelly bean guessing game is a metaphor that reveals how far off you can be if you're making uninformed decisions about your money.

How much interest will you pay over the life of your car loan or home mortgage?

How much life insurance do you need to protect your family financially?

How much do you need to have saved for the future, and are you on track?

If you're not on track, at what age will your money run out?

How much will Social Security pay you each month?

How much monthly income will your 401(k) provide, and at what age will it run out?

If you can't answer questions like these, you may be like so many others who assume there will always be enough and hope everything will turn out OK.

How is that possible? A lifetime of wild guesses and blissful ignorance explains why so many people facing retirement panic when they see how little they'll be forced to live on for the rest of their days.

Is this true for you? If so, you could be just like TJ...

"Wow! I thought it'd be a whole lot more."

Ouch.

Put Your Guesses to the Test

Over the life
of your car loan...

...how much will you pay in interest?

Guess: $ _____

Actual: $ _____

Over the life
of your mortgage...

...how much will you pay in interest?

Guess: $ _____

Actual: $ _____

At your current rate
of saving...

...how much will you have by age 67?

Guess: $ _____

Actual: $ _____

Based on how much money
you will need each year
in retirement...

...at what age will you run out of money?

Guess: _____

Actual: _____

It's time to face it. You're a sucker.

Does that offend you? Good, it should. Let it be a wake-up call. When you don't know how money works, you can be taken advantage of time and time again.

You're a sucker. Own it and you've taken the first step toward not being one.

Being financially illiterate sucks. But the following key concepts will help you transition from sucker to student and from student to master. The whole point of learning how money works is never to be fooled again. Not by banks. Not by credit card companies. Not by online offers. Not by employers. Not by family or friends. Not even by the number one person in your life responsible for making money—YOU!

Knowing beans about money is worth a lot more than bragging rights. It could mean living your best life today, realizing the dreams you have for yourself and your family tomorrow—and helping others do the same.

Now that we've covered the realities about money, roll up your sleeves and grab a jar of jelly beans. It's time to discover...

Three money concepts every sucker should know.

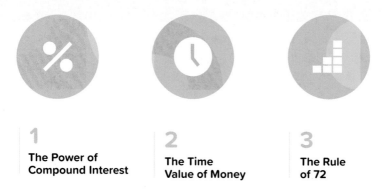

1
**The Power of
Compound Interest**

2
**The Time
Value of Money**

3
**The Rule
of 72**

How the sucker thinks.

"I'm saving a little. I've got that retirement thing
at work. And there's always Social Security.
That'll be enough, right?"

How the wealthy think.

"Preparing for the future is my responsibility.
That means I've got to get with it,
get informed, and get it done."

What have you learned?

Your future is too important
to be left to a _____.

It's critical to know
the most important _____
regarding my money.

OK... I can admit it.
We're _____.

Mei: wild guess
TJ: numbers
Sarah: suckers

1 | CONCEPTS

The Power of Compound Interest

The power of compound interest refers to the growth potential of money over time by leveraging the magic of "compounding," which is interest paid on the sum of deposits plus all interest previously paid.

Whoa! So it's like interest on interest.

Exactly! Gold star, Zoey.

Before you can appreciate the power of compounding, you must discover the power of interest.

John D. Rockefeller was America's first self-made billionaire.[9] At the time of his death in 1937, he was worth over $340 billion in today's money.

How rich is that? If you combined the wealth of Warren Buffett, Bill Gates, and Jeff Bezos, Rockefeller would still be richer. We're talking hard-to-imagine rich. Think Scrooge McDuck doing back strokes in his money vault—but even richer.

But before he became a mega-wealthy oil tycoon, Rockefeller grew up in a humble country home in upstate New York. During his youth, he learned a pivotal lesson about how money works. At 14 years old, Rockefeller had saved up $50 ($1,500 in today's money) selling turkeys and doing chores for neighbors.

Like many 14-year-old boys, young Rockefeller received some shrewd advice from his mother. She encouraged him to lend his $50 to a local farmer. It was arranged that the money would be paid back in 12 months with 7% interest. A year later, the farmer made good on the deal, returning to Rockefeller the $50 plus $3.50 in interest.

It was around this same time that a neighbor hired Rockefeller to dig potatoes for three days. Rockefeller was paid $1.12.

Rockefeller's New York Times obituary said that "on entering the two transactions in his ledger he realized that his pay for this work was less than one-third the annual interest on his $50, and he resolved to make as much money work for him as he could."[9]

What if every 14-year-old learned this pivotal lesson and resolved themselves to make as much money work for them as they could? Many, however, never do. Instead, they end up "digging up potatoes" their entire lives.

Unlike Rockefeller, they never really discover the power of interest and how to put their money to work to build a future they could never earn with their hands.

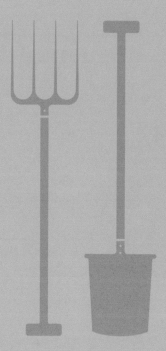

You working for your money

The number of hours in the day limit
how much you can earn.

Your money working for you

There is no limit on how much you can earn
because your money grows independently
from your personal efforts.

"

I have ways of making money you know nothing of.

– JOHN D. ROCKEFELLER

Ugh! What an elitist quote!
That's just... scary.

Seems to me like this kinda info is
too important to be kept secret.
Everyone should have access to it.

66

As of 2018, 51.2% of the Earth's population is now online.[10]

– INTERNATIONAL TELECOMMUNICATION UNION

That makes NOW the perfect time in history to teach people how money works.

I reckon that's the whole point of this book. No more secrets.

Simple Interest vs. Compound Interest

Let's take the Rockefeller lesson about putting your money to work a little further. What if the farmer wanted to borrow the money for more than one year?

Rockefeller and the farmer could have agreed on simple interest or compound interest.

To see the difference, let's convert Rockefeller's $50 loan into today's money —roughly $1,500. And let's imagine that the 14-year-old Rockefeller and the farmer agreed on 9% annual interest and a 50-year term. Rockefeller would get his loan back plus interest around retirement age.

If Rockefeller and the farmer chose simple interest, the farmer would only pay interest on the original loan amount every single year.

Simple Interest Example

How this chart works:

- It represents a 50-year timeline

- 9% simple interest is paid on the $1,500 original loan amount annually

- Notice that growth is relatively flat because the interest paid is the same each year

$140,000

$105,000

$70,000

$35,000

$1,500 $8,250

Year   0 2 4 6 8 10 12 14 16 18 20 22 24 26 28 30 32 34 36 38 40 42 44 46 48 50

Compound interest blows simple interest away.

As you can see from the simple interest example, it's not a very attractive way to put your money to work. Which is why bank accounts and savings vehicles don't typically offer simple interest. Compound interest is standard. Here's why...

Let's return to our previous example of Rockefeller lending $1,500 to the farmer for a 50-year term at 9% interest. But instead of simple interest, what if Rockefeller and the farmer agreed that interest would compound annually.

Every year, the farmer would owe Rockefeller interest on both the original amount of the loan—the $1,500 principal—and ALL the interest that had accrued from prior years. With interest earning interest, Rockefeller's money would be working a lot harder. How much faster would his money have grown with the power of compounding?

Compound Interest Example

How this chart works:[11]

- The chart represents a 50-year timeline

- 9% annual interest is paid on the $1,500 original loan amount, compounded monthly

- Notice how growth increases more and more rapidly as interest compounds

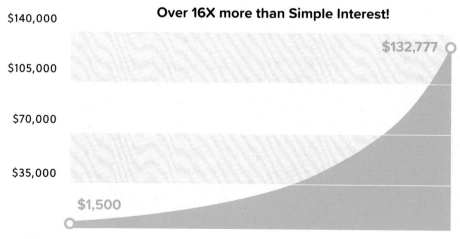

Over 16X more than Simple Interest!

$140,000

$105,000 — $132,777

$70,000

$35,000

$1,500

Year 0 2 4 6 8 10 12 14 16 18 20 22 24 26 28 30 32 34 36 38 40 42 44 46 48 50

"

Compound interest is the greatest mathematical discovery of all time.

— ALBERT EINSTEIN

Did he really say that? I thought that was an urban myth.

Haha. Maybe it was Yogi Berra who said it...

Yogi Bear? What does a cartoon have to do with compounding?

Hey, guys... mind if we get back on track here?

Saving with compound interest beats savings alone.

When people save money, they're often thinking more about keeping that hard-earned money safe, rather than how to put it to work with compound interest. Look below to see how savings add up compared to how savings earning compound interest add up.

How this chart works:[11]

- An account is opened with $500

- Each month, $500 is added to the account

- For 45 years, the money compounds monthly at a 9% constant annual interest rate

- Notice that it's the interest earned that creates significant growth, not the savings added

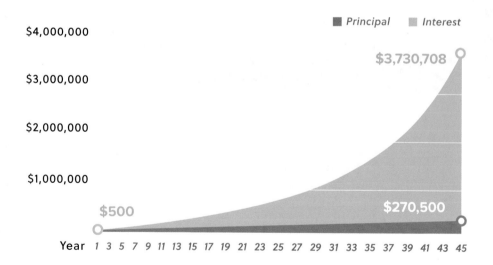

You only added $270,500 to the account, but in 45 years, it's worth $3,730,708! That's $3,460,208 in interest! The interest is almost 13X the amount you put in!

Saving money every month always makes a difference.

Let's say that one day Sarah opens a savings account with $50,000 but never adds another dime to the account. On the same day, TJ opens the exact same type of account with $500 and then adds an additional $500 every month. Both accounts earn a constant 9% annual interest rate.

After 45 years, whose account is worth more—Sarah's or TJ's?

How this chart works:[11]

- Sarah starts with $50,000 but never adds any more money

- TJ starts with $500 and adds an additional $500 every month

- They both earn a constant 9% annual interest rate, compounded monthly

- The term is 45 years

$4,000,000

$3,730,708 — ○
TJ's Total

$3,000,000

$2,826,829 ———— ○
Sarah's Total

$2,000,000

TJ Adds
$50,000 $500/mo. ——
Sarah's Start

$1,000,000

$500
TJ's Start

Year   0 2 4 6 8 10 12 14 16 18 20 22 24 26 28 30 32 34 36 38 40 42 44

With only $500 at the start, TJ earns more! Regardless of how much you have to start with, consistent savings each month can make a big difference.

Compounding and time count. But what about interest rates—does that matter? Oh, yeah!

Take a look at the growth curves below. They each reflect $178 added each month to a monthly compounding account beginning at age 25 and then growing until age 67. Observe how significant the difference the spike in growth can be when your interest rate is just a few percentage points higher. Compounding, time, and your interest rate all influence how hard your money can work for you.

Once you see the difference, it's hard to imagine intentionally placing money at 3% or 1% or less, yet it happens every day.

How this chart works:[11]

- Assumes $178 is added each month from age 25 to age 67

- Assumes a 1%, 3%, 6%, or 9% average annual interest rate, compounded monthly

- Based on a retirement age of 67

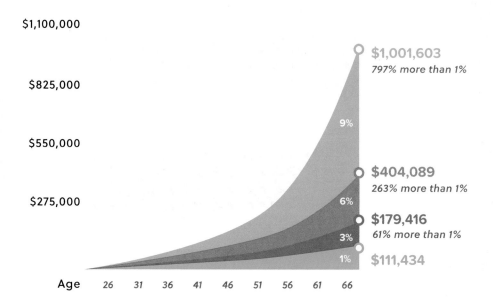

$1,100,000

$825,000

$550,000

$275,000

9%

$1,001,603
797% more than 1%

$404,089
263% more than 1%

6%

$179,416
61% more than 1%

3%

1% $111,434

Age   26   31   36   41   46   51   56   61   66

How the sucker thinks.

"I've worked hard for my money so I just want to put it away and keep it as safe as possible."

How the wealthy think.

"I've worked hard for my money so now it's going to work for me, as hard as possible."

What have you learned?

Compound interest is
_____ earning _____.

Saving is prudent. But savings
that earn _____ interest
is superlative.

Getting the _____ interest
rate possible can make all the
difference in the world!

George: *interest, interest*
Mei: *compound*
Hector: *highest*

2 | CONCEPTS

The Time Value of Money

The time value of money is the concept that money available to you now is worth more than the same amount in the future because of its potential to earn interest.

In other words, money saved today is worth more than money saved tomorrow.

 Exactly! Great job, TJ.

It's so warm.

66

It ain't much I'm asking,
if you want the truth.
Here's to the future.
Hear the cry of youth.
I want it all, I want it all,
I want it all and I want it now.

– QUEEN

Time is money, especially when the time is now!

Queen's anthem nails the mindset of the sucker perfectly.

Every corner of society offers instant gratification and immediate enjoyment with a pain-free purchase. Feel the impulse to shop? Your favorite brand has an app for that. Time to pay taxes? File at turbo speed. Owe a friend cash? Square it away with a text. Even today's churches let you tithe with a tap.

Have you ever asked yourself why everyone wants to make it so easy for you to spend your money? Is it...

A. Because they value you? (Come on, you're not that naive.)

B. Because they value your money? (Getting closer.)

C. Because they want your money, they want it all and they want it now!

Of course, the answer is "C." Make no mistake, we live in an ASAP world. You've been conditioned to want everything ASAP because they want your money ASAP.

Every dollar you own has a little stopwatch inside. The sooner you press the start button, the sooner each dollar can start earning interest. Money you put to work today has the potential to earn more interest than money you put to work tomorrow. Why? Because it has more time to grow. Those who know how money works never want to waste a single day of earning potential.

Did you think it was a coincidence that taxes are taken out of paychecks now but tax refunds are not paid until the next year? Ever wondered why financial companies hold funds for a few days rather than release them to you immediately?

Could it be the same reason that marketers beg you to ACT NOW? They want it all and they want it now—but if they owe it to you, they'll pay it only after they've squeezed out every possible day of earning.

They're not doing anything wrong. They're just taking full advantage of the time value of money. It's time you did too.

Tick tock! When it comes to money, time is precious.

Another way to think of the time value of money is in terms of how many years you have left to grow your savings.

Let's do some reverse engineering. Think about how many years you have left until...

You pay off your car loan or home mortgage.
Your kids go to college.
You retire.
Your savings run out in retirement.

Don't freak out. Knowing those numbers creates urgency and urgency drives action. Now we're getting somewhere. Take a breath and consider the...

3 Time-Tested Actions to Leverage the Time Value of Money

1. Start Now

NOW is always the best time to start.

2. Save Regularly

Get the highest interest rate possible.

3. Be Patient

Good things come to those who wait.

Think'n back, I didn't start save'n regularly and patiently until I was about 30. Would it have made that much of a difference if I'd started in my early 20's?

Important question, George.
Let's take a look at that...

Starting earlier can make a significant difference!

It's true. Saving less earlier can crush saving more later. Look at this scenario with Sarah and George—both saving for retirement. Sarah starts at 22, but stops saving when she's 30. George starts saving at 30 and continues until retirement age. Both earn a constant 9% annual interest rate, compounded monthly.

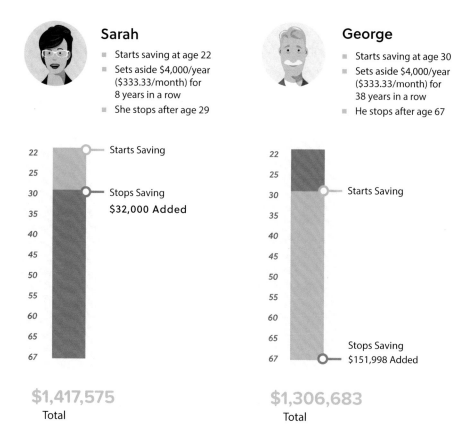

Sarah
- Starts saving at age 22
- Sets aside $4,000/year ($333.33/month) for 8 years in a row
- She stops after age 29

George
- Starts saving at age 30
- Sets aside $4,000/year ($333.33/month) for 38 years in a row
- He stops after age 67

Sarah chart:
- 22 — Starts Saving
- 30 — Stops Saving, $32,000 Added

$1,417,575
Total

George chart:
- 30 — Starts Saving
- 67 — Stops Saving, $151,998 Added

$1,306,683
Total

Sarah has $110,892 more!

George puts away 4.75X more money than Sarah, but Sarah has more money in the end. All because she started saving earlier.[11]

Goodness gracious. I'm not 22 anymore. I'm 49. How much would I need to save monthly to have $1 million by my late 60's?

At your age, Sarah, you'll need to save about $2,000 monthly.

The longer you wait to start saving, the more you need to come up with every month. Locate your age in the chart below to see how much you'll need to put away. Notice how much less it would be if you start younger or how much more if you wait.

How much do you need to save to hit $1 million by retirement?

How this chart works:[11]

- Find your age to see how much you'll need to save monthly and daily
- Assumes a 9% average annual interest rate, compounded monthly
- Based on a retirement age of 67

AGE	MONTHLY AMOUNT	DAILY AMOUNT	AVERAGE INCOME[12]	% OF INCOME NEEDED
20	$113/mo.	$4/day	$1,413/mo.	8%
25	$178/mo.	$6/day	$3,123/mo.	5.7%
30	$282/mo.	$9/day	$4,263/mo.	6.6%
35	$451/mo.	$15/day	$4,818/mo.	9.4%
40	$731/mo.	$24/day	$5,569/mo.	13.1%
45	$1,212/mo.	$40/day	$5,548/mo.	21.8%
50	$2,088/mo.	$69/day	$5,638/mo.	37%
55	$3,880/mo.	$128/day	$5,924/mo.	65.5%
60	$8,589/mo.	$282/day	$5,505/mo.	156%

Why didn't someone show us this when we were younger?

The more useful question is, what do we do about it now?

For one thing, I'm telling every 20-year-old I know.

Let's look at your numbers. (Remember, no wild guesses.)

What's your current age?

Based on the chart on the previous page, how much do you need to start saving each month to have about $1 million by retirement age?

What's the monthly amount if you wait 5 years?

Name a few people you'd like to show the chart to next.

What if every parent understood the power of compounding and the time value of money?

According to the Department of Agriculture, the average cost to raise a child is $233,610.[13] What if parents put aside just a fraction of that amount for each child before birth? $13,000 works well, as we'll see in a moment. If parents scraped, scrounged, worked extra hours, asked relatives for assistance—whatever it took —what could that do for a child's future? And how much would a child lose if parents waited until after high school graduation to put away the money?

What if you put away $13,000 for each of your children?

How this chart works:[11]

- Assumes a one-time lump sum of $13,000 is put away

- Timeframe 1 shows the account growth for 67 years, starting at birth

- Timeframe 2 shows the account growth for 49 years, starting at age 18

- Assumes a 6.5% average annual interest rate, compounded monthly

Timeframe 1—A one-time $13,000 lump sum that grows from birth to age 67

$13,000 $1,000,442

Birth   *Age 67*

Timeframe 2—A one-time $13,000 lump sum that grows from age 18 to age 67

$13,000 $311,486

Age 18   *Age 67*

Here's another way you could accomplish the same objective by putting away a smaller lump sum plus a monthly amount.

If wrangling $13,000 before a child is born isn't feasible, parents can still leverage the power of compound interest and the time value of money. They could simply take a more incremental approach starting the month the child is born, putting $2,500 down and adding $250 every month for 4 years.

What if $2,500 was put down and $250 was added every month for 4 years for each of your children?

How this chart works:[11]

- Assumes a one-time lump sum of $2,500 and $250 monthly for 4 years

- Timeframe 1 shows the account growth for 67 years, starting at birth

- Timeframe 2 shows the account growth for 49 years, starting at age 18

- Assumes a 6.5% average annual interest rate, compounded monthly

Timeframe 1—$2,500 + $250 per mo. for 4 yrs that grows from birth to age 67

$2,500 + $12,000*　　　　　　　　**$1,008,059**

Birth　　　　　　　　　　　　　　　　　*Age 67*

Timeframe 2—$2,500 + $250 per mo. for 4 yrs that grows from age 18 to age 67

$2,500 + $12,000*　　　　　**$313,857**

Age 18　　　　　　　　　　　　　　*Age 67*

*$250 x 48 months

A Solution to One of Society's Greatest Financial Blunders

One of the greatest financial blunders of society is dismissing the first two decades of a child's life as nothing more than a giant expense to parents. Instead, those years should be recognized for what they are—a valuable financial resource for the child. Capitalizing on these squandered decades is perhaps the most affordable, realistic way for parents to retire their children as millionaires.

Which of these 3 scenarios is most likely to be possible?

1. Leave a $1 million inheritance
2. Set aside $13,000 at birth
3. Set aside $2,500 at birth + save $250 per month for 4 years

Each of the three scenarios could create a million dollar foundation by retirement, but 2 and 3 are less costly by far. Why? Because they leverage the power of compound interest and the time value of money. Your financial professional can help you design a plan for each of your children or grandchildren.

The sucker, who won't even have enough money for their own retirement, hopes in vain to leave their children a small inheritance. The wealthy remove the need for an inheritance by transforming their child's early years to earning years.

It's perhaps the most overlooked financial advantage of all time. It's one that almost every parent has missed. It could single handedly wipe out the number one fear of retirees, which is not illness or even death—it's running out of money.

It's time that parents start maximizing the time value of money for each of their children, starting no later than birth. It's time society as a whole made this shift.

I don't mean to rain on the parade, but how do you prevent the children from touching that money until they're 67?

That's what trusts are for, Sarah. They hold and protect the money until the appointed time.

According to data from the United Nations, 250 children are born in the world every minute.[14] Imagine how different their lives would be if every family created a savings plan for their children that couldn't be touched until retirement age.

Looks like P.T. Barnum was way off—it's 250 suckers that are born every minute.

Ha! Good one, George.

WOW! This would give children greater freedom to explore, fail, and find their purpose throughout their lives all because their parents took this one revolutionary step for them.

You start saving before you start walking. I love it! It's like every child's born a million dollar baby.

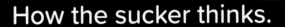

How the sucker thinks.

"I know saving is important, but now's just not a good time for me to deal with it."

How the wealthy think.

"Here's the deal. Time is money. Every day counts. Building my financial future starts NOW."

What have you learned?

Due to its growth potential, money I have _____ is more valuable than money I have _____ .

Because _____ matters, I need to start saving as _____ as possible!

Knowing how much to save at my current _____ will help me nail my goals for retirement.

Dana: today, tomorrow
Sarah: time, soon
TJ: age

3 | CONCEPTS

The Rule
of 72

The Rule of 72 is a mental math shortcut—a simple, powerful formula that can be used to quickly approximate the amount of time it takes for money to double, given a fixed annual rate of interest.

Cha-CHING! So this magic formula will help me double my money?

No. But it can help you estimate how many years it will take for your money to double.

What good is that?

And... do I still get a gold star?

As you'll see, it's quite useful. Sorry, buddy. No gold star.

Basket Case—Every bank's little inside joke... on you.

What do you find in the little basket on the counter of every bank? You guessed it—suckers. You can't make this stuff up. It's like their little inside joke. Delighted that you've walked right in not knowing how money works, they offer a free sucker with a smile. Don't believe it's intentional? What brand are the suckers? You're a dumb-dumb if you miss that one.

OK. Total mind freak. But hold on.
A moment ago, you told me to leverage
the power of compound interest.
Savings accounts earn interest.
So why would bankers smile when
I leave with a sucker? I don't get it...

In the chapter, The Power of Compound Interest, you learned to leverage compounding—but ALSO that your rate of interest matters. Here's where that comes into play...

In 2019, the national average interest rate on savings accounts was 0.09%.[15]

After you deposit your money into your savings or checking account, what does the bank do with it? They lend it to other customers in the form of loans, like car loans and home mortgages. And what do you think is the national average interest rate on those types of loans? Car loans are over 6%.[16] Home mortgages are over 4%.[17]

So let's do the math. Your money earns you 0.09%. But they use YOUR money to earn 4-6%. Does that seem fair? You get safety. But they get rich. What a deal... for them.

Now you know why they smile, Clark. ⟩

There's almost $10 trillion stagnating
in savings accounts averaging
only .09% annual interest.[18]

Yeah, but .09% is better
than nothing, right?

Legitimate question, TJ. Let's dig a little deeper...

The Rule of 72 attacks the false perception of growth.

Let's break this down. There are three main reasons why people stash so much money in low interest savings accounts. One, they want their money to be safe. Valid reason. Two, they want easy access to their money. Also valid. Three, they think their money is growing.

This third reason is the one that should trigger a red flag. For many, the actual rate of return almost doesn't matter. The fact that the account offers interest at all can fool consumers with the false perception of growth.

The false perception of growth describes the sucker's misconception that their money will one day accrue into something substantial. They don't stop to estimate if the growth rate aligns with their savings goals, because they've never been taught **HOW** to estimate it.

Enter, the Rule of 72. Your gleaming sword that can slash the false perception of growth and help you conquer your savings goals.

Swords
are cool.

Yeah, they are.

The Rule of 72 is a mental math shortcut.[19]

It's a simple formula that can be used to approximate the number of years it will take for your money to double. Sound like math? It is. But making music and getting home from Mars also require math, and both of those are pretty great. So stop being a sucker and follow along. (It's really, really easy.) Here's how it works...

Divide 72 by your interest rate. The result is the number of years it will take your money to double.

72 ÷ interest rate = years to double

That's all there is to it. Congratulations. Now you know the Rule of 72.

Plug in your interest rate to see how many years until your money will double. The shorter the time, the better.

So on my calculator, for a 6% interest rate, I hit 72, then divide by the number 6. That gives me 12 years... it worked!

$72 ÷$

1 % =	**72**	years to double
3 % =	**24**	years to double
6 % =	**12**	years to double
9 % =	**8**	years to double
12% =	**6**	years to double

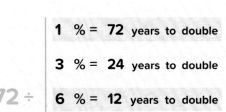

Give the Rule of 72 a try.

Do you have any of the accounts or debts below? Plug in your interest rate to estimate how many years before money doubles—for you... or for someone else.[19]

Accounts (Money doubling for you)	Interest Rate		Years to Double
Savings/Money Market Account	72 ÷	%	=
401(k)/IRA/CD	72 ÷	%	=
Indexed Fund	72 ÷	%	=
Mutual Fund	72 ÷	%	=

Debts (Money doubling against you)	Interest Rate		Years to Double
Credit Card Debt	72 ÷	%	=
Car Loan	72 ÷	%	=
Home Mortgage	72 ÷	%	=
Student Loan	72 ÷	%	=

The question is, whose money is doubling faster, yours... or theirs?

Bingo! Gold star, Clark.

The more time you have, the more "doubles" you get.

Think about your savings for the future. The Rule of 72 can give you an idea of how many doubles you'll get in your lifetime.[19] With more time, a lower interest rate may give you enough to nail your goals. With less time, you may need a higher interest rate.

Look at the nest eggs below. Notice the huge difference in doubles between 3% interest and 12% interest at 48 years of growth.

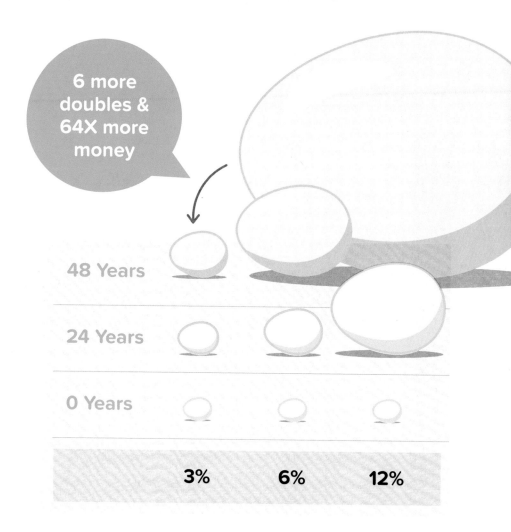

Every percentage point matters. Every double counts.[19]

I'm 19 and I just received a $10,000 inheritance. If I wanted to grow it to $1 million by retirement, how many doubles and what interest rate do I need?

Look below, Zoey. You'd need more than 9% interest and almost 7 doubles to reach $1 million by age 67.

AGE ▼	1%	3%	6%	9%	12%
19	$10,000	$10,000	$10,000	$10,000	$10,000
					$20,000
				$20,000	$40,000
31					
			$20,000	$40,000	$80,000
43		$20,000		$80,000	$160,000
					$320,000
			$40,000	$160,000	$640,000
61					
				$320,000	$1,280,000
67	$16,000	$40,000	$80,000	$640,000	$2,560,000
Retirement	‹1 double	2 doubles	4 doubles	6 doubles	8 doubles
	doubles every 72 years	doubles every 24 years	doubles every 12 years	doubles every 8 years	doubles every 6 years

The Rule of 72 works the other way too.

Instead of starting with your interest rate to calculate how many years it will take for your money to double, you can go the other way. You can start with the number of years you have left to save to find the interest rate you'll need to reach your savings goals.

In this case, you divide 72 by the number of years you have left to save. The result is the interest rate you need for your money to double within that time frame.[19]

72 ÷ years left to save = interest rate needed

I have a $500,000 retirement account and I'm 57 years old. Are you saying that if I want my money to double to $1 million by retirement, which is 10 years from now, I can divide 72 by 10 to get the interest rate I need?

Precisely, Mei. You'd need a 7.2% rate of return. See below...

72 ÷ 10 years left = 7.2% interest rate needed

The national average
interest rate for savings
accounts is .09%.[15]

72 ÷ .09% = 800 years

800 years!

For reference, 800 years ago the Crusades were
underway, Genghis Khan was crowned, and the
Magna Carta was signed.

Do you want to wait that long
for your money to double?

Compare that to the national average interest rate for credit cards, which is over 17%.[20]

$$72 \div 17\% = 4.2 \text{ years}$$

4.2 years!

A sucker will wait 800 years for their money to double, while others, like credit card companies, figured out how to get a double every 4.2 years.

That's like battling Genghis Khan's army. It's not a fair fight!

Which is why this knowledge is so critical, Mei. It levels the playing field... or battlefield.

The Rule of 72 is more than a cool math trick.

It's a practical eye opener that forces you to ask shrewd questions before making important money decisions.

Here are some of the questions you'll be compelled to ask...

Is a bank account the best place to put my money? Am I willing to settle for a 1% or even a 2% rate of return? Or is there a way I can get a 4% or 6% return—or perhaps even higher?

What type of higher interest accounts still provide adequate safety?

Can I finance or refinance my car loan or mortgage with a lower interest rate?

Will the financial institution managing my money earn more interest than I will?

Will I get enough "doubles" during my income-earning years to reach my savings goals for retirement? If not, what do I need to change?

> ## Suckers don't ask these kinds of questions. They're not even really aware that to grow their money—at some point —it has to double!

When you know the Rule of 72, you're less likely to fall for gimmicky promotions from banks, settle for opportunities that don't give you the advantage, and take on debt that might take forever to pay off.

When you know the Rule of 72, you're more likely to pause and run that useful little calculation:

72 ÷ interest rate = years to double

Smile back at them

Now that you know the Rule of 72, you know the deal with banks. But don't get cocky. They're always thinking of slicker ways to get your money and save their costs.

The banking world has gone mobile. In fact, 72% of people in a recent study prefer banking online instead of visiting a local branch.[21] Deposits are "direct" or done with a couple of taps on an app. It's all about getting your money faster to generate more compound interest than ever before. With online banking, they even found a way to save the cost of the sucker basket.

But now you've got their number.

Next time you visit a bank, skip the free sucker and smile back at them.

Your future is no longer their inside joke.

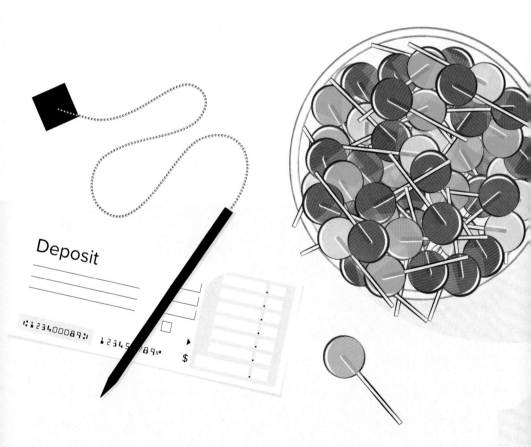

How the sucker thinks.

"The Rule of 72 sounds like math. Boooring!"

How the wealthy think.

"Math rocks! The Rule of 72 is simple, powerful, and practical."

What have you learned?

The Rule of 72 helps you estimate when your money will _____.

Divide 72 by your _____ to approximate how many years it will take for your money to double.

With low interest checking and savings accounts, it's likely that the _____ is earning more interest with your money than you are.

Clark: double
Zoey: interest rate
TJ: financial institution

The 7 Money Milestones

to Financial Security and Independence

The 7 Money Milestones are the key steps that will help you achieve financial security, become financially independent, and pursue wealth by overcoming debt, protecting and prioritizing income, developing savings, growing cash, and guarding your financial legacy.

Sounds comprehensive,
I hope it's also easy...

Nothing good comes easy, Hector.
The 7 Money Milestones are straightforward,
time-tested, and worth it.

Fair enough.
Bring it!

The 7 Money Milestones: Your roadmap to financial security and independence.

Congratulations! Training camp is over. Things are about to get real. Remember—what we think about, we bring about. Now you know how to stop being a sucker and start thinking like the wealthy.

You're ready to make decisions with confidence. It's time to take all your dreams for the future and start bringing them about—one step at a time.

The 7 Money Milestones give you a roadmap to get from where you are today—however lost you may feel—to the summit of financial security and independence.

Thinking like the wealthy, however, means not going it alone.

Find a financial professional to help you complete the milestones. Every journey needs a guide to help navigate the twists, turns, and forks in the road. You'll share the victories along the way and the view from the top. Don't start without choosing yours.

A few tips the wealthy would give you before you set out...

- There will never be a perfect time to get started, so **START NOW!**
- Completing ALL the milestones is more important than completing them in order.
- Expect setbacks, but don't lose heart. **KEEP GOING!**

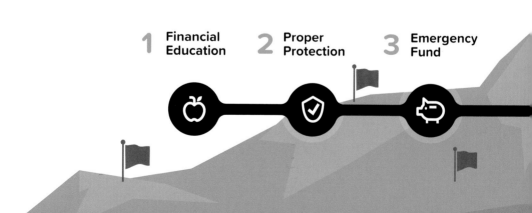

1 Financial Education
2 Proper Protection
3 Emergency Fund

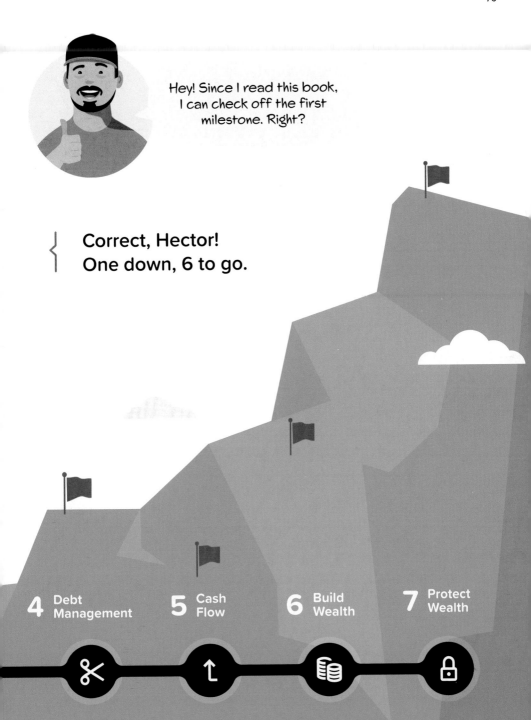

Hey! Since I read this book, I can check off the first milestone. Right?

Correct, Hector!
One down, 6 to go.

4 Debt Management

5 Cash Flow

6 Build Wealth

7 Protect Wealth

"

Without local guides, your
enemy employs the land
as a weapon against you.

– SUN TZU

MILESTONE 1
Get a Financial Education

In the war for your money, there are two weapons you'll need to win. Both are inexpensive. One is having a solid foundation for your financial education. Second is an experienced guide—one who can provide continuing education and industry resources when it's time to make key decisions about your money and your future.

This book and the entire HowMoneyWorks® program is your foundation. But you still need someone to help you navigate life's financial twists and turns. Find a financial professional you trust to fight by your side.

The knowledge you've gained in this book will help protect you from being a sucker ever again. It's time for you and your financial professional to put everything you've learned to work. It's time to make the move from the basket of suckers to the summit of financial security and independence.

Make it a top priority. Find your financial professional. Complete the milestones.

Dana, you're a
smarty pants.
Can I get'cha to be
my financial pro?

You're sweet George,
but you need someone
licensed and trained.
So do I.

MILESTONE 2

Secure Proper Protection

The famous writer and revolutionary, Thomas Paine, once wrote, "The protection of a man's person is more sacred than the protection of property."[22] Certainly, self-preservation is paramount. But here's the thing. You might not be able to fully protect yourself from illness or accidents. But you can protect your income and your wealth. Ironically, protection of your financial assets is called "life insurance." It's a defensive strategy motivated by a sense of love, responsibility—or both.

Along with obtaining a financial education, proper protection of your income should be the first milestone to complete. Why? Because without your ability to provide for your family or your business, stability they enjoy today could become hardship they can't overcome tomorrow.

To secure proper protection for all those who depend on you, sit down with your financial professional to have a conversation about life insurance as soon as possible. Already have life insurance? When was the last time you had a review?

Keen advice, but are there certain words
I should be familiar with before my review?
I always like knowing the jargon.

{ Sure, Mei. Here's a short list...

Key Life Insurance Terminology

Owner: The person who controls the rights to the policy and pays the premium

Insured: The person whose life is covered

Insurer: The company that pays the death benefit if the insured dies

Beneficiary: The person(s) who receives the death benefit when the insured dies

Premium: The payments made by the owner to the insurer

Death Benefit: The money paid to the beneficiary

How do I calculate the amount of insurance I need? Is there a rule of thumb I can use as a starting point?

Yes, Dana. Generally speaking, life insurance should cover 10X your annual family income.[23]

Using the rule of thumb that you need 10X your annual family income, an individual who earns $50,000 per year should have $500,000 of life insurance. Likewise, if you earn $100,000, you should have $1,000,000 of coverage.

You and your financial professional will calculate your needs together since everyone's situation is a bit different. The factors you'll consider include...

- Age
- Debt
- Income/current financial situation
- Health
- Number of dependents
- Role in your business

You and your financial professional should discuss questions like these:

- What are your short-term and long-term debts, loans, and goals?
- How much is your mortgage or rent payment?
- How old are your children? How much will their education cost?
- Do you have any assets to help cover funeral costs, like an emergency fund?

I looked at life insurance options once before and got overwhelmed. How do I pick the right one?

All life insurance falls into two categories, TJ. Temporary and Permanent. Let's look at them both...

Temporary (aka Term) Life Insurance

Temporary life insurance provides protection for a specified period of time, like 10, 20, or 30 years. You get it for a "term"—which is why it's known as "term life insurance." It's the most affordable life insurance available because it provides one core feature—a death benefit—and because it expires after the term.

With term life insurance, it's possible to secure a substantial amount of financial protection for your family or business with a relatively small monthly payment. This can make it a fit for those with limited budgets during times of high financial responsibility, like the following...

 Raising children
Protect your family from the high cost of child care

 Owing a mortgage
Protect your family from the burden of home loan payments

 Paying for college
Protect your family from the burden of tuition debt

 Running a company
Protect business partners from the cost of filling your role

There's no replacing you. But term life insurance can help your family replace the income you provided and your business partners replace the role you filled. It's inexpensive life insurance that safeguards families and businesses financially for set periods of time.

Temporary (Term) Life Insurance

PROTECTS YOUR FAMILY OR BUSINESS FOR A SET PERIOD, LIKE 10, 20, OR 30 YEARS, DURING TIMES OF HIGH FINANCIAL RESPONSIBILITY

What happens when the term ends?

Term insurance is a foundational tool to secure proper protection for your family or business. But what happens when the term ends? There are two basic scenarios...

Scenario 1—You no longer need term life insurance
If your children are grown and independent and their education and your home are paid off, your financial responsibilities may have decreased to a point that you don't need a term policy and you can let your policy end.

Scenario 2—You still need term life insurance
After your first term, you may still have a mortgage, you may be a single income couple, you may have grown children or grandchildren at home, or your business may continue to rely on you. For these reasons and more, you may wish to purchase a new term policy. First, however, you must qualify medically. If you don't qualify, a new term policy may not be an option. If you do qualify, the new policy will cost more. The older you are, the more expensive term life insurance will be.

Important note: Some term policies offer "guaranteed insurability," which means the insurance company won't turn you down for a new policy due to medical reasons. Expect policies that offer this benefit to cost more.

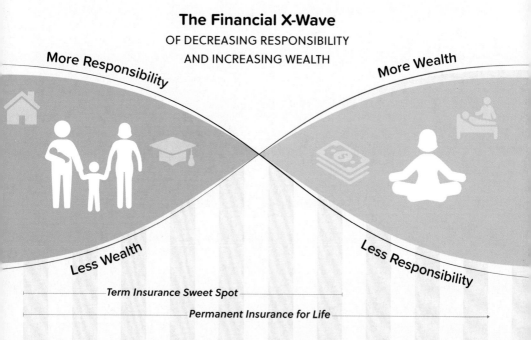

The Financial X-Wave
OF DECREASING RESPONSIBILITY
AND INCREASING WEALTH

More Responsibility

More Wealth

Less Wealth

Less Responsibility

Term Insurance Sweet Spot

Permanent Insurance for Life

Permanent Life Insurance

Like term, permanent life insurance provides a death benefit to protect your family financially; however, it's designed to be kept for life—not just a term. It also offers more benefits, which is why it costs more. Think of permanent life insurance as a lifelong strategy that can protect your family today, secure your wealth in the future, and provide for your heirs after you're gone.

Important Benefits

You get life insurance coverage for life. As long as you don't let your policy expire, you will never lose your insurance due to illness or health problems.

You can add long-term care protection as an optional rider. Long-term care protection can help cover the costs of services you're likely to need one day, like in-home care or a nursing home. You can add long-term care protection for an extra cost by coupling it with your permanent life insurance policy.

You have flexibility with your premium. After you've accumulated cash value in your policy, it can be used to cover the cost of insurance if you can't pay your monthly premiums for a while. This flexibility can help prevent a lapse of coverage.

Permanent Life Insurance

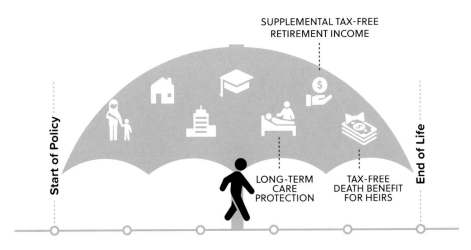

PROTECTS YOUR FAMILY FOR THE REST OF YOUR LIFE AND CAN OFFER
A RANGE OF ADDITIONAL BENEFITS YOU'RE LIKELY TO NEED DOWN THE ROAD

What can the cash value of permanent life insurance do for you?

If you're like many, you're not just unfamiliar with the concept of cash value —you may have never heard of it. Cash value is by far the most pivotal benefit of permanent life insurance after the death benefit. It's simple and powerful.

Here's how it works. A portion of your monthly premium is set aside in an account that grows over the life of your policy. Different policies calculate the growth of your cash differently. Some pay you a guaranteed interest rate while others offer growth tied to a variety of investment markets. Either way, you're activating a benefit of your life insurance policy that leverages the power of compound interest.

Cash value can be used to fund purchases like a new car, a vacation, or even a wedding. And at some point, often around the age of 65 or 70, you can "throw the switch" on your policy. At this time, you can start taking out tax-free income for retirement, as long as the policy value is sufficient.[24]

Powerful Advantages of Cash Value

Tax-Free Growth—You never pay tax on the growth of your money as it compounds over the life of the policy.

Zero Market Risk—Normally, money tied to the market is exposed to both gains AND losses. However, some permanent life insurance policies make it possible to take advantage of gains tied to the market while completely avoiding losses.

Creditor-Free—In most states, the cash value associated with a permanent life insurance policy can't be touched by creditors.[25]

Tax-Free Income—When you decide to take money out of your policy to use as income or make purchases, you never pay tax on it as long as the policy is active.

It seems term and perm serve different purposes. Would it behoove me to have both?

It could, Mei. That's a common strategy.

Wow! Life insurance can do so much.

But it's also like the greatest proof of love you can give your family.

You guys obviously never had my Fire-in-the-Hole Chili. That recipe is the greatest proof of my love. Every one of my dadgum relatives is waiting for me to drop dead so they can finally get their hands on it.

Accurate. I've tasted it. It's a culinary treasure.

I get how life insurance protects me financially. But, like, what if my wife or I suffer from Alzheimer's or dementia? Wouldn't the cost of a nursing home wipe me out? How do I protect my family from that?

Pretty sure that's what health insurance is for, Hector.

Incorrect, Sarah. Hector's instincts are on point. Health insurance, including Medicare, covers medical bills. Medicaid is only for people who are essentially broke. Disability insurance covers loss of pay. Long-term care insurance is the protection Hector is referring to. And chances are, you will need it at some point in your life.

70%

of people age 65 and over will need some type of long-term care services and support in their remaining years[26]

8%

of people over age 55 have purchased long-term care insurance coverage[27]

You're being confusing. Are you saying that to secure proper protection, I need life insurance AND long-term care insurance?

That depends, Sarah. Those are important options to discuss with your financial professional.

Long-Term Care Insurance

Long-term care (LTC) insurance helps cover out of pocket expenses for qualified long-term care services, including nursing home care, home health care, assisted living care, and adult day care.[28]

My Grandma Rosa could have used this! It's for older people who can't get out of bed, get dressed, or feed themselves, right?

Anyone at any age could be like Rosa, Hector. In fact, 37% of people who receive LTC benefits are under the age of 65.[26]

Because you never know at what age you might need long-term care, consider securing LTC insurance when you're younger and healthier—when it's most affordable and easiest to qualify for.

The average LTC need—if more than one year—is 3.9 years.[29] How would you recover from bills that could pile up into the hundreds of thousands of dollars?

Long-Term Care Type[30]	ANNUAL MEDIAN COSTS	AVERAGE TOTAL COST
Adult Day Health Care	$18,720	$73,008
Assisted Living Facility *(private, 1 bedroom)*	$48,000	$187,200
Home Health Aide Services	$50,336	$196,310
Nursing Home *(semi-private room)*	$89,297	$348,258
Nursing Home *(private room)*	$100,375	$391,463

Which option to purchase LTC insurance would you pick?

Option 1—Purchase LTC insurance as a traditional, stand-alone policy
Even if you don't have life insurance, you can go directly to an insurance company to purchase a stand-alone LTC insurance policy. With this option...

- While stand-alone LTC policies start off with low premiums, insurance companies often raise rates on existing LTC policies.[31]

- With many policies, you pay out of pocket for care and then get reimbursed after submitting receipts.

- The 90-day waiting period for benefits that most LTC policies require can be customized for stand-alone policies by paying a higher or lower premium.

- Since there's a 70% chance you'll need LTC, there's a 30% chance you won't. You could spend thousands on premiums and get nothing in return.[32]

Option 2—Add LTC protection as a rider to a permanent life insurance policy
If you're planning to get permanent life insurance, you can add LTC protection to the policy in the form of a rider for an extra cost. With this option...

- Unlike stand-alone LTC policies, life insurance companies typically don't raise rates for policy holders.

- Some insurance companies pay you money to cover LTC expenses— after the waiting period—which you can spend as you see fit. No need to submit receipts once eligibility requirements have been met.

- You can get significant savings by coupling your life and LTC protection.

- If you're one of the lucky 30% who won't need LTC, your premiums aren't wasted. Instead, your family receives a tax-free death benefit.

Two Other Living Benefit Riders to Consider

Besides LTC insurance, there are other living benefit riders to consider adding to your permanent life insurance policy.[33] Some are quite affordable or cost nothing extra to add. Here are two popular living benefits to consider...

Critical Illness—This rider enables the insured, who is diagnosed with a critical illness, like a heart attack, stroke, or cancer, to collect a portion of their death benefit to cover expenses.

Chronic Illness—If the insured is diagnosed with a chronic illness, like ALS, Alzheimer's disease, arthritis, or diabetes, this rider enables the insured to access a portion of their death benefit.

MILESTONE 3
Create an Emergency Fund

Even the most conscientious budgeter will eventually face an unexpected financial blow. Think about the three little pigs. The first two made their homes from hay and sticks. They were suckers—totally unprepared for the inevitable wolf. But you're not a sucker anymore. Your emergency fund is like the house made of bricks, ready for the wolf to huff and puff.

To prepare for life's big bad wolves, you're going to set up an emergency fund. It's a designated stash of cash at your fingertips to help you recover from unforeseen expenses without derailing your financial strategy or depleting your savings account.

I don't have a lot of cash just lying around. Where do I get the money to create an emergency fund?

You'll put away a little money every month until you have about 3-6 months of income saved, TJ.

It's recommended to have 3 to 6 months of your income in your emergency fund. This gives you precious breathing room in case of missed work, medical bills, property damage, broken appliances, surprise IRS fees—you name it. If you're currently living paycheck-to-paycheck, like many people are today, your emergency fund could be the insulation that separates you from financial disaster.

As you work towards your 3-6 month emergency fund, start by making your first goal 2 weeks of pay. Then 1 month, then 2, until you reach your goal.

With your emergency fund in place, you're no longer broke. Way to go!

THE 2 RULES OF AN

Emergency Fund

Rule #1

Your emergency fund is ONLY for unexpected
emergencies. That's all. It's not for last minute birthday
presents, much needed spa days, or irresistible Black
Friday sales. It doesn't matter if it sits in your checking,
savings, or a separate account—as long as it doesn't
tempt you to use it for anything but a true emergency.

Rule #2

If you need to use your emergency fund to fix a car,
replace the fridge, or pay for braces, take the money
and spend it. That's what it's for. Just make sure that
afterwards you add back a little money every month
until your emergency fund is full again.

MILESTONE 4
Apply Debt Management

With financial protection in place and your emergency fund in the works, it's time to face your debt. For many, it is THE greatest obstacle to a sound financial future and becoming financially independent. Debt is a sweeping crisis perpetuated by a society of suckers led astray by the instant-gratification desires of our generation. That's a mouthful—but it's true.

I'm in my 30's and I owe on my student loans and credit cards. Am I the only goofball here still in debt?

I must be a goofball too, Clarky-boy. Still work'n down a few credit cards myself.

It pains me to admit this, but I have a pesky balance on an old store credit card... Make that three goofballs.

You're courageous to admit it, crew. You're also not alone...

80% of all American adults are in debt,[34] and over half of Americans own a credit card. The average credit card debt per household with a credit card is $8,284.[35]

How do you get out of debt? Suckers buy lottery tickets. Fools wait for a miracle. But people who know how money works take responsibility and face debt head-on. It takes determination, focus, accountability—AND a sound strategy defined by you and your financial professional. Get started with these tips.

5 Tips to Eliminate and Stay Out of Debt

 Know What You Owe—Make a list of all your credit card debts and loans and write down your outstanding balance, interest rate, monthly payment, and monthly due date for each. Once a year, pull your credit report from a free online service. Make sure it's accurate. Check out the websites of the top credit agencies for pointers on how to report and correct the errors.

 No More Late Payments—Paying after the due date hurts your credit score and accrues late fees. Sign up for automatic payments or set alarms on your phone so you're never late again.

 Target One Debt at a Time—If you have balances on multiple credit cards, pay down the total balance one card at a time. Pay off the card with the smallest balance or the highest interest rate first. Whichever one you target, pay more than the minimum—as much as possible within your budget. After zeroing out the first one, start on the next smallest balance or highest interest rate card. Add the money you were paying on the previous card to your payment on the next one. Repeat the process until you're credit card debt free.

 Stop Charging and Cancel Unused Subscriptions—Stash credit cards in a safe place and stop using them. Use cash or check cards/mobile pay services that pull from your actual checking account balance. Then cancel all unnecessary subscriptions like online memberships and video streaming services that sink you further in debt each month.

 Refinance Your Mortgage—By paying on time, correcting credit report errors, and reducing debt, your credit score should improve. In time, you may qualify for a more favorable interest rate or type of loan on your home.

MILESTONE 5

Increase Cash Flow

Cash flow is the money you have available to spend or to save. After you have established financial protection, an emergency fund, and a debt strategy, you're in a position to focus on your cash flow, which can help you eliminate debt and grow savings faster. The key to cash flow is examining, managing, and reducing expenses.

Consider the following techniques:

- Create and stick to a budget by weighing income vs. expenses and needs vs. wants

- Develop a written game plan to spend less than you earn

- Raise deductibles on your auto and homeowners policies to help lower premiums

- Reposition money that's currently sitting in low interest savings accounts

- Drop Private Mortgage Insurance (PMI) as soon as the equity in your home reaches 20% of your home's value

I've budgeted and I'm frugal. What can I do to improve cash flow if I'm just plumb stuck?

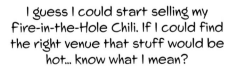

There's almost always a way to get unstuck, George.

I guess I could start selling my Fire-in-the-Hole Chili. If I could find the right venue that stuff would be hot... know what I mean?

3 Practical Options to Get Your Cash Flow Unstuck

1. Get a Side Gig

Earning additional income is almost always a quicker way to reach your financial goals than just trying to spend less. A recent survey found that 45% of U.S. workers have a side gig earning an average of $1,122 per month.[36]

There's like a million ways. I make extra cash with an app that's like Uber for dog walking. Seriously. People pay me to walk their dogs.

I started selling sandwiches on my weekends. Boom! Now I have a dozen food trucks. Hey, George, how 'bout I try your chili out in my trucks? Let's make it happen!

2. Start a Business

Low cost business opportunities are out there. By becoming an entrepreneur part-time, you could leverage hours outside of your day job. As income increases, you can choose the moment to transition away from employment to full-time with the business.

3. Adjust Your W-2 Allowances

Some people celebrate receiving a big refund check from the IRS every year. If that's you, consider this. By adjusting your W-2 allowances, more of your cash could be in your paycheck all year long instead of the IRS's bank account. Consult with your tax advisor before making this change.

I run a hospital. Our HR department conducts a staff workshop on this tactic. It's helped a number of our teammates save more and increase their 401(k) contributions to max out our company match.

MILESTONE 6
Build Your Wealth

Will your wealth last as long as you do? It's a question you **MUST** be able to answer.

American transcendentalist, Henry David Thoreau, said "Wealth is the ability to fully experience life." But he was only half right. In the 21st century, wealth may also be a matter of financial survival.

As you accumulate assets along life's way, you may be fortunate enough to enjoy your wealth, share it with others, and leave it as part of your legacy. Today, however, wealth has another role that could be essential for you. It may be a necessary asset to fund a very long retirement—which could be an eye-popping 30 years or longer.

For many who have saved little to date, growing wealth may seem like pie in the sky. But it should be a commitment to get serious about as soon as possible. Knuckle down with your financial professional to begin your asset accumulation strategy so you can build wealth for both quality and longevity of life.

63% of people have a greater fear of running out of money in retirement than dying.[37]

For couples who make it to retirement age, there's a 50% chance that one spouse will live past 95 and a 25% chance that one will live past 96.[38]

So it's a coin toss to make it to your 90's now. That's a pretty good shot.

A 20-30 year retirement is exciting, but, yeah—that'll take a lot of money.

Whatever stage of life you're in, start building wealth now!

It's flawed thinking that wealth is something you start building "when you have money." It's classic Sucker Cycle thinking. "I'll start saving after I get that raise" and "once my savings account grows a bit, I'll figure out what to do with it" are foolish notions. This is why so many remain trapped in a loop of spending too much and saving too little. The wealthy, on the other hand, stopped the spending early on, started saving, and put whatever money they had available to work. The difference is getting started wherever you are and developing the discipline to save.

The secret to breaking the Sucker Cycle is paying yourself first. That means you apply the concepts of this book, decide how much you can put away, and then deposit that money into savings and investment accounts—*before* you buy a latte, go to a movie, split a pizza, or even pay your bills.

Hold up. You pay yourself first even before you pay your bills?

You still pay your bills, Zoey. It just means you budget in savings first, then bills, and whatever is left over can be spent. You're prioritizing the necessities of the future over the impulses of the present.

4 Disciplines That Promote Wealth Building

Save regularly by automating direct deposits	Don't touch your savings until you reach your goal	Review goals and progress at least once a year	Make adjustments as your life and finances change

Do these with your financial professional

The 4 Threats Every Wealth Builder Must Conquer

Now that you know the disciplines that help build wealth, it's time to confront the biggest threats that can thwart your wealth building efforts. If you don't know how they work or how to deal with them, they can prevent you from reaching your goals or force you to rethink your retirement plans altogether.

1. **Procrastination**—You're now well aware of the time value of money and that the time to save is always NOW. The sucker skips through life, putting off money tasks for another day. And when her son needs tuition, his daughter wants a wedding, or retirement looms on the horizon, oh how they wish they could go back in time and do something more.

2. **Inflation**—Over the last 100 years the cost of goods increased by an average of 2.8% each year due to inflation.[39] If you estimate that you need $1 million to live comfortably in retirement and you plan to retire in 25 years, you'd be in for a shock. If you base your estimate on the cost of goods today and if the average rate of inflation remains the same, your calculation would be off by over half. In other words, you would need almost $2 million for retirement—not $1 million.

3. **Losses**—Between the years 2000 and 2010, the stock market lost around 50% of its value—twice.[40] Those years of losses devastated families who were counting on consistent gains to meet their investment goals. It's wise to heed the words of famed investor, Warren Buffett, who said, "Rule number one, never lose money. Rule number two, never forget rule number one." Strategies to shield your wealth from the loss of principal are available and should not be overlooked.

4. **Taxes**—Sales tax doesn't sneak up on you—it's right there on the receipt. Income tax, on the other hand, can rear its ugly head decades later. Imagine being blindsided in your late 60's that you owe 20% or 30% tax on your $1 million nest egg. Poof! That's $200,000 or $300,000 gone. Whether your future ends with a tax strategy—or tax tragedy—can depend on the financial vehicle and the tax structure you choose today.

Now that you know the threats, it's time to review strategies that can help conquer them. Then discuss this critical Money Milestone with your financial professional.

" "

Procrastination is, hands down,
our favorite form of self-sabotage.

— ALYCE CORNYN-SELBY

I'm going to read this
section as soon as I
beat this level.

You put the "pro" in
procrastinate, Clark.

The Impact of Procrastination

Failing to save and invest money because you lack education is one thing. Failing to save and invest because you're lazy… that's another. These two excuses are like Bonnie and Clyde, working together to rob suckers of the future they could have.

Procrastination kills wealth. It's why Americans, in a recent survey, confessed to paying $3 billion in credit card late fees.[41] It's why 50% of people who don't have a will say "I just haven't gotten around to it."[42] And it's why 85% of Americans don't have a financial professional, who would typically meet with them at no charge.[43]

5 Actions to Overcome Financial Procrastination

1. Read this book at least twice—education removes the paralyzing effect of fear
2. Find a financial professional and schedule a meeting this week
3. Use the 7 Money Milestones, and set specific goals and deadlines for each
4. Work the Milestones as a team with a partner, spouse, parent, or trusted friend
5. Post goals and deadlines where you'll see them daily (closet, mirror, or bedroom)

The Impact of Inflation

Think of inflation as the tax of time. The annual inflation rate has averaged 2.8% for the last 100 years.[39] How many years does it take the cost of goods to double at a steady 2.8% annual inflation rate? It's time to put the Rule of 72 to work!

Formula: 72 ÷ Average Inflation Rate = Years Until The Cost of Goods Doubles

Result: 72 ÷ 2.8 = 25.7 Years[19]

In 25.7 years, a $5 burger could cost $10—a $200,000 home could be $400,000. Inflation is a major factor to consider when planning for the future. Here are two tips to prepare for the tax of time…

1. Using average annual inflation rates, base your retirement income needs on what goods may cost in the future, not on what they cost now.
2. Start a business selling goods and services that you can maintain throughout retirement, which can give you an income stream that rises with inflation.

The Impact of Losses

Suppose you lost 50% of a $10,000 investment.

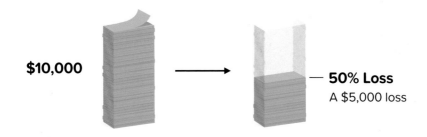

$10,000

— **50% Loss**
A $5,000 loss

To get back to $10,000, would you need a gain of 50% or 100%?

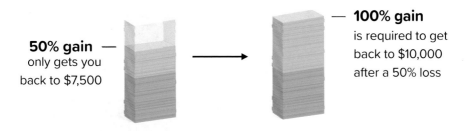

50% gain —
only gets you
back to $7,500

— **100% gain**
is required to get
back to $10,000
after a 50% loss

The years between 2000 and 2010 are referred to as the lost decade. During this span, the stock market lost 50% of its value twice. Years of gains vaporized. Nest eggs vanished. Dreams evaporated. Major setbacks like these—and even minor losses—can throw off your savings goals and dash your plans for the future.

3 Strategies to Protect Against The Impact of Losses

1. Reduce the risk of losses by picking investments with lower risk. Unfortunately, the rate of return on these investments is typically low.

2. Diversify your portfolio across different types of investments in multiple industries with varying degrees of risk. This strategy is called diversification.

3. Utilize financial vehicles tied to investment markets that allow you to benefit from the gains, but eliminate the risk of losses.

Don't procrastinate. Consider inflation. And talk with your financial professional about ways to reduce—or remove—the impact of losses from your strategy.

The Impact of Taxes

You pay taxes to federal and state governments on your salary, wages, and income on an annual basis. This section is not about that. It focuses on how earnings from various savings and investment vehicles are taxed. When you know how these taxes work, you're better equipped to make decisions with your financial professional about which strategies are the most advantageous for you.

The 3 Different Ways Savings and Investment Accounts Are Taxed

Tax Now (Taxable)
With accounts of this type, you pay taxes on interest, earnings, and dividends every single year.

Examples
• Stocks & Bonds
• Mutual Funds
• Savings Accounts
• Certificates of Deposit (CDs)

Tax Later (Tax-Deferred)
With accounts of this type, you're not taxed until you start taking distributions in retirement.

Examples
• Traditional IRAs
• 401(k)s & 403(b)s
• Annuities

Tax Never (Tax-Free)
With accounts of this type, your earnings and distributions are never taxed.

Examples
• Roth IRAs
• Permanent Life Insurance
• Municipal Bonds
• College Savings Plans

The Seed vs. The Harvest

One of the big questions to answer is when you want to pay taxes. Consider this example: If you save $10,000 at age 29 and earn a 9% annual return each year, you would have $250,000 when you reach 65. Would you rather pay taxes on...

The Seed
Paying tax on the initial $10,000 means only your principal will be taxed, not your earnings—and you'll pay today's tax rate.

The Harvest
Paying tax on the $250,000 harvest means all your earnings will be taxed—and you'll pay the future tax rate, which could be higher.

How Taxes Affect Various Savings & Investment Accounts[25]

Taxable Accounts

With taxable accounts, you make an investment with money that has already been taxed—income you've earned from your business, or salary and wages from employment. You pay taxes annually on the interest and dividends your accounts earn unless held in qualified retirement plans.

Qualified Retirement Plans

With 401(k), 403(b), 457, and IRA plans, your pre-tax dollars grow without having to pay taxes on the principal or growth until retirement, at which time, you'll pay income tax at the future tax rate on the full amount of distributions each year.

Annuities

Money invested in an annuity—except for qualified retirement plans—will have already been taxed. The growth in an annuity is tax-deferred until retirement. At that time, you'll pay income taxes on the growth portion of your distributions each year.

Government Bonds

You use after-tax money to invest in government and municipal bonds (excluding qualified retirement plans). The interest on federal government bonds is taxable at the federal level, but not at the state and local level. Conversely, the interest on municipal bonds is exempt from federal income tax. If you live in the state in which the municipal bond is issued, you can also avoid state and local taxes.

Roth IRAs

You invest in a Roth IRA with after-tax dollars. Your account grows tax-free and you don't pay taxes on distributions in retirement. Unfortunately, the IRS limits the use of Roth IRAs to people below a specific income level and restricts the annual amount they can add to their accounts.

Permanent Life Insurance

Premiums are paid with after-tax dollars. As long as your policy remains active, you will never pay taxes on distributions you take for supplemental retirement income or special purchases. Distributions, however, will reduce your death benefit. The IRS doesn't limit the annual amount you can contribute or restrict income levels for eligibility, which is why permanent life insurance is often referred to as the "Roth IRA for the wealthy."

> 66
>
> Everyone has a plan until they get punched in the mouth.
>
> – MIKE TYSON

"THEN DON'T GET IN THE RING WITH MIKE TYSON, DUH"

~ CLARK

Amiright?

You couldn't be more right, Clark. Avoiding the threat of running out of money makes a lot of sense.

Avoid the Risk of Running out of Money in Retirement

Guaranteed Income

Company pensions are all but obsolete. Employees now rely on a combination of 401(k) plans and Social Security benefits to provide enough money to live on in retirement. The average 60 to 69-year-old American only has $195,500 in their 401(k).[44] The average income of 65-year-olds is $48,685.[45] That's almost exactly a fourth of their 401(k) balance. So how many years will their 401(k) last?

Let's say you only live on 50% of the $48,685 income you had before retiring—that's $24,343 per year. If you factored in 2.8% inflation and you could get a 6% annual return on your 401(k) account which is worth $195,500, you would run out of money in approximately 9 years.[46] That means if you started taking distributions at age 67, your 401(k) would be gone by age 76. What if you lived until you were 85 or 95? Will Social Security alone be enough?

When your retirement income isn't guaranteed, you've left yourself open to getting punched in the mouth. That's why you "don't get in the ring," just like Clark said.

> # In a recent Gallup survey,[47] 85% of non-retired American investors strongly agreed that having a guaranteed income stream in retirement to supplement Social Security benefits is critical.

You know the behaviors for building wealth. And you're aware of the threats. But making your wealth last as long as you do can seem like a bigger challenge than building it. This is especially true with retirement now lasting two or three decades—or even longer. So how do you begin?

Start by working with your financial professional to calculate your probability of running out of money based on your current financial trajectory. Then, you can explore options to establish a reliable monthly retirement income you can depend on while you still have time to do something about it.

MILESTONE 7

Protect Your Wealth

Aretha Franklin died in 2018 with an estate worth over $80 million. Prince's assets were valued over $150 million when he died in 2016. Both left their families and business partners with an emotional, financial, and legal mess that would take years to sort out. Why? Because neither had an estate plan.

No one would want to call The Queen of Soul and His Royal Badness suckers— but you have to wonder what they were thinking. How could you have accumulated that much wealth and not have a plan for it in the event of your untimely death? Were they like so many others who just never took the time?

> ## The #1 reason Americans give for not having a will is that "they just didn't get around to it."[42]

Aretha Franklin and Prince are just two recent examples of notable people from history who "didn't get around to it." Pablo Picasso, Howard Hughes, Sonny Bono, and Abraham Lincoln were all found intestate (without a will at death).

Your estate is made up of everything that belongs to you—your house, cars, furniture, electronic devices, personal possessions, checking and savings accounts, investments, life insurance, and business ownership. Also included are the guardianship of your underage children and debts you owe.

Almost everyone has an estate and almost everyone believes having an estate plan is important. Many, however, think their estate is too small to merit an estate plan or they're convinced getting one would be too expensive.

> ## 76% of Americans agree that having a will is important, but nearly half of older Americans don't have a will or estate plan.[42]

It's like they say, "you can't take it with you when you go so don't leave a clean up on aisle 3."

Nope. No one says that, Clark.

Your estate plan is how you protect your wealth, your family, and your legacy when you die or if you're incapacitated. It's the set of documents used by your loved ones to carry out your wishes and decisions.

4 Documents Your Estate Plan Should Include[25]

 Will

Identifies who will be the guardian of your minor or special needs children, who you want to carry out your wishes, and how you want your property distributed

 Financial Power of Attorney

Gives your spouse or other trusted person control over your financial affairs, like paying your bills, insurance, taxes, or selling your property, if you're not able to do it yourself

 Advance Healthcare Directive or Living Will

Identifies the person you want to make your healthcare decisions if you cannot and states what medical treatment you wish to receive if you're unable to choose

 Health Insurance Portability and Accountability Act (HIPAA) Release

Permits your healthcare agent to legally access your medical records and insurance information to facilitate your medical treatment

If your intentions are never formalized in an estate plan, a court may be the one to decide how your property is distributed and who will be your children's guardian. The process of a court administering an estate in accordance with state laws is called probate. It's an ordeal that can be long, expensive, and take a heavy toll on those who depended on you.

Even if you have a will, many of the assets titled in your name must go through the probate process before your heirs can receive them. And if you own real estate in other states, your estate may require multiple probates.

You can help your family and business partners avoid unnecessary expenses and delays of the probate process with one additional estate planning tool.

It's called a trust. It can...

- Manage your property after you become physically or cognitively impaired
- Protect the interests of your children who are currently incapable of handling money due to age, immaturity, disability, illness, or substance abuse
- Protect special needs children and beneficiaries from losing eligibility for government benefits
- Provide privacy since the trust is not filed with the probate court
- Avoid probate in multiple states if you own real estate in more than one state
- Lower your estate taxes and provide added tax advantages for large estates

Does this mean everyone needs a trust? They sound expensive.

Not everyone, TJ. But if you do, it could be a bargain compared to the legal costs your family might owe one day.

Keep this in mind, some assets pass directly to your named beneficiaries at death and are not transferred through a will or trust, including life insurance, annuities, IRAs, 401(k)s, or other qualified retirement plans. Some bank and investment accounts distribute funds directly to named beneficiaries. Also, jointly owned assets with right of survivorship pass directly to the joint tenant at death.

Think it will be too expensive or time-consuming to get your estate plan done? Then you haven't considered the cost and time it could steal from your loved ones down the road if you don't. From local attorneys to online services, there are options for almost every budget. There's no good reason to delay checking this final Milestone off the list. Do it immediately.

Your next step is to put ink on paper.
Or, rather, info on paper.

Your HowMoneyWorks Money Discovery begins now.

Yes, it's time to fill out a form. But this isn't your run-of-the-mill form, like you fill out at the DMV or chiropractor.

This is THE form—the one that kicks off the 7 Money Milestones and helps your financial professional help you define your goals.

It can change the course of your future.

No, really.

It's that big a deal.

Your
HOWMONEY**WORKS**®
Money Discovery

How the sucker thinks.

"I like figuring things out on my own. Thanks, but I got this."

How the wealthy think.

"I want the confidence and freedom these milestones and a trusted professional can give me. Thanks, I'm on it."

What have you learned?

A financial education gives me a solid _____ to build upon.

Since I've read this book, I only have _____ milestones left to complete. I can do this.

Before I complete the 7 Money Milestones, the first action is to start working with a _____ who can help guide me.

Dana: foundation
Hector: 6
George: financial professional

Your HOW MONEY WORKS® Money Discovery

Name(s)	DOB	Phone	Annual Income	Bonus

Address

Name of dependent(s)	Age	Name of dependent(s)	Age

Goals

	Short-Term 1-3 Years	Mid-Term 3-7 Years	Long-Term 7+ Years
Build retirement wealth			
Create guaranteed retirement income			
Buy new home			
Set up emergency fund			
Fund education			
Support parents			
Start a business			

Financial Questions

End-of-the-month amount you can allocate to goals

Do you want a complimentary analysis of options that could help you maximize Social Security income?

Yes   No

Previous year's tax refund

Do you have a will and/or a trust?

Yes   No

Existing college plans

Do you have a long-term care policy?

Yes   No

If applicable, what are your parents' plans for long-term care?

Do you have a pension?

Yes   No

Life Insurance

Insured	Company	Type	Amount	Cash Value	Premium	Year Issued

Assets

	Tax Now			Tax Later			Tax Never	
	BALANCE	MONTHLY CONTRIB.		BALANCE	MONTHLY CONTRIB.		BALANCE	MONTHLY CONTRIB.
MUTUAL FUNDS			ANNUITIES (FIXED / VARIABLE)			ROTH IRA		
BROK. ACCTS. / STOCKS / BONDS			TRAD. IRA / SEP IRA			CASH VALUE LIFE INSURANCE		
CHECKING / SAVINGS / CD'S			401(K) / 403(B) / OTHER QUAL. PLAN			EMPLOYER MATCH		

Other

Any other assets or expenses to consider? (expected inheritances, child w/ special needs, etc.)

Behind the Creative

Andy Horner

Andy is the CEO of Outstand, a hybrid software and creative services company. He and his team have helped clients build their brand, tell their story, and serve their clients with world-class design and digital tools for over 12 years. Andy is a graduate of Virginia Commonwealth University, where he studied Communication Arts and Design. Before starting his own company, he led creative at a variety of ad agencies and web design studios. Today, Outstand offers a wide range of software and creative services, from marketing campaign management and brand development to web design and video production. A storyteller at heart, Andy develops a series of graphic novels for teens in his spare time. He lives in Atlanta, Georgia with his wife, Tonia, and their 4 sons.

About the Authors

Tom Mathews

Tom is a 38-year veteran and co-founder of one of the largest financial services organizations in North America. He's been a champion for middle-income families, helping them access financial services and education that had been predominantly available only to the wealthy. Tom has made a career of bringing high-tech to high-touch. From starting one of the first financial industry websites and making laptop computers mainstream in 1993, to podcasts and streaming television shows today, he has always been a pioneer. A native of Cincinnati, Ohio, Tom has a degree in Accounting from Xavier University and is the author of "Aim For The Heart, Leading to Build Great Teams." He now resides in Atlanta, Georgia and oversees 450 offices with a team of over 8,000 financial professionals. An accomplished trumpet player and music aficionado, Tom and his wife, Cindy, have two daughters and one granddaughter.[48]

Steve Siebold

Steve is the author of "How Rich People Think," "Secrets Self-Made Millionaires Teach Their Kids," and "Get Tough/Retire Rich." Since 1984, Steve has interviewed over 1,300 self-made millionaires around the world, which has been recognized as the largest study ever conducted of the self-made rich. Steve has been a featured guest on The Today Show, Good Morning America, CNBC, Fox News Channel, and hundreds of other television shows, websites and publications across the world. His concepts and writings are cited in top online publications throughout the web each week. His books have sold over 1.2 million copies and have been translated into 6 languages. A guitarist—and collector of guitars—Steve is a native of Chicago, Illinois, and now resides in Atlanta, Georgia with his wife, Dawn.

Resources and Disclosures

1. "What is Financial Literacy and Why Should You Care?," Mark Catanzaro, Apr 2019, stlouisfed.org/open-vault/2019/april/what-is-financial-literacy-why-care

2. "The New Social Contract: a Blueprint For Retirement in the 21st Century —The Aegon Retirement Readiness Survey 2018," Aegon—Center for Longevity and Retirement, May 2018, aegon.com/contentassets/6724d008b6e14fa1a4ced b41811f748a/retirement-readiness-survey-2018.pdf

3. "4 Stats That Reveal How Badly America Is Failing At Financial Literacy," Forbes, Apr 2018, forbes.com/sites/danipascarella/2018/04/03/4-stats-that-reveal-how-badly-america-is-failing-at-financial-literacy/#78647d922bb7

4. "Survey Shows How Much Money Americans Feel Financial Literacy Shortfalls Cost Them in 2018," PR Newswire, Jan 2019, prnewswire.com/news-releases/survey-shows-how-much-money-americans-feel-financial-literacy-shortfalls-cost-them-in-2018-300775623.html

5. "Financial Literacy Statistics," National Financial Educators Council, Mar 2019, financialeducatorscouncil.org/financial-literacy-statistics/

6. "Survey of the States: Economic and Personal Finance Education in Our Nation's Schools 2018," Council for Economic Education, Feb 2018, councilforeconed.org/wp-content/uploads/2018/02/2018-SOS-Layout-18.pdf

7. "What is 'Retirement'? Three Generations Prepare for Older Age," Transamerica Center for Retirement Studies, 19th Annual Transamerica Retirement Study of Workers, Apr 2019, transamericacenter.org/docs/default-source/retirement-survey-of-workers/tcrs2019_sr_what_is_retirement_by_generation.pdf

8. "New Survey Finds Americans' Spending Habits Are Ruining Their Retirement," Cameron Huddleston, Jan 2019, finance.yahoo.com/news/survey-finds-americans-spending-habits-100000015.html

9. "The New York Times Book of the Dead: Obituaries of Extraordinary People," edited by William McDonald, 2016, books.google.com/books?id=mDmKC wAAQBAJ&pg=PT384&lpg=PT384&dq= %22on+entering+the+two+transaction s+in+his+ledger%22+Rockefeller&sou rce=bl&ots=dg2aI1cOj-&sig=ACfU3U3- -Ja_#v=onepage&q=%22on%20 entering%20the%20two%20 transactions%20in%20his%20 ledger%22%20Rockefeller&f=false

10. New ITU statistics show more than half the world is now using the internet," ITU News, Dec 2018, news.itu.int/itu-statistics-leaving-no-one-offline/

11. This is a hypothetical scenario for illustration purposes only and does not represent an actual investment in any product. Actual investments can fluctuate in value and there is no assurance that these results can or will be achieved. It does not include performance risks, expenses, fees or taxes associated with any actual investment, which would lower results. Rate of return is an assumed constant nominal rate, compounded monthly. It is unlikely that any one rate of return will be sustained over time. Investing entails risk, including possible loss of principal. Numbers are rounded to the nearest dollar in some cases. Retirement needs vary by income and cost of living—$1 million isn't an adequate goal for every saver.

12. "Income Percentile by Age Calculator for the United States in 2018," PK, Oct 2019, dqydj.com/income-percentile-by-age-calculator/

13. "The Cost of Raising a Child," U.S. Department of Agriculture, 2017, usda.gov/media/blog/2017/01/13/cost-raising-child

14. "With 250 babies born each minute, how many people can the earth sustain," *Guardian*, 2018, *theguardian.com/global-development/2018/apr/23/population-how-many-people-can-the-earth-sustain-lucy-lamble*

15. "Average Bank Interest Rates in 2019: Checking, Savings, Money Market, and CD Rates," ValuePenguin, 2019, *valuepenguin. com/banking/average-bank-interest-rates*

16. "New-car loans hit highest interest rates in a decade," Claudia Assis, MarketWatch, Apr 2019, *marketwatch.com/story/new-car-loans-hit-highest-interest-rates-in-a-decade-2019-04-02*

17. "Mortgage rates tumble as one economist waves the white flag," Andrea Riquier, MarketWatch, May 2019, *marketwatch. com/story/mortgage-rates-tumble-as-one-economist-waves-the-white-flag-2019-05-02*

18. Savings Deposits (including money market deposit accounts) $9.5 Trillion as of Aug 5, 2019, Table 4, *federalreserve.gov/releases/h6/current/*

19. The Rule of 72 is a mathematical concept that approximates the number of years it will take to double the principal at a constant rate of return compounded over time. All figures are for illustrative purposes only, and do not reflect the performance risks, fees, expenses or taxes associated with an actual investment. If these costs were reflected, the amounts shown would be lower and the time to double would be longer. The rate of return of investments fluctuates over time and, as a result, the actual time it will take an investment to double in value cannot be predicted with any certainty. Investing entails risk, including possible loss of principal. Results are rounded for illustrative purposes. Actual results in each case are slightly higher or lower.

20. "Rate survey: Average card APR remains at 17.71 percent," Kelly Dilworth, Aug 2019, Rate Report, August 2019," Kelly Dilworth,

Aug 2019, *creditcards.com/credit-card-news/rate-report.php*

21. "Survey: Online, Mobile are Most Popular Banking Channels, Branches Remain Popular," American Bankers Association, Oct 2018, *aba.com/Press/Pages/101618MCResults.aspx*

22. "Dissertation on First-Principles of Government.," Thomas Paine, 1795, *quod.lib.umich.edu/e/ecco/004809392.0001.000/1:2? rgn=div1;view=fulltext*

23. There are many variables that affect your life insurance needs. You may need more or less insurance depending on any existing savings, assets, retirement funds and whether the purpose of the death benefit is to replace income or for estate planning.

24. Loans, withdrawals, and death benefit accelerations will reduce the policy value and death benefit. Provided the policy is not and does not become a modified endowment contract (MEC), 1) withdrawals are tax-free to the extent that they do not exceed the policy basis (generally, premiums paid less withdrawals) and 2) policy loans are tax-free as long as the policy remains in force. If the policy is surrendered or lapses, the amount of the policy loan will be considered a distribution from the policy and will be taxable to the extent that such loan plus other distributions at that time exceed the policy basis.

25. HowMoneyWorks does not provide tax or legal advice. Please consult with your personal tax and/or legal professional for guidance on your particular situation.

26. "The Basics," LongTermCare.gov, Oct 2017, *longtermcare.acl.gov/the-basics/*

27. "The State of Long-Term Care Insurance: The Market, Challenges and Future Innovations," National Association of Insurance Commissioners, May 2016, *naic.org/documents/cipr_current_ study_160519_ltc_insurance.pdf*

28. Long term care coverage is subject to policy limitations, an elimination period, and other requirements.

29. "Long Term Care Statistics," LTC Tree, Dec 2018, *ltctree.com/long-term-care-statistics/*

30. "Genworth Cost of Care Survey 2018," *genworth.com/aging-and-you/finances/cost-of-care.html*

31. "States try to beat back rate increases on long-term-care policies," InvestmentNews, Sep 2018, *investmentnews.com/article/20180913/FREE/180919958/states-try-to-beat-back-rate-increases-on-long-term-care-policies*

32. "How Much Care Will You Need?," Oct 2017, *longtermcare.acl.gov/the-basics/how-much-care-will-you-need.html*

33. Accelerating the death benefit reduces the value of the policy. The actual benefit paid to the policy owner will be less than the amount that is accelerated.

34. "It's Official: Most Americans Are Currently in Debt," Maurie Backman, Feb 2018, *fool.com/retirement/2018/02/15/its-official-most-americans-are-currently-in-debt.aspx*

35. "Key Figures Behind America's Consumer Debt," Bill Fay, 2019, *debt.org/faqs/americans-in-debt/*

36. "One-third of Americans say they need a side gig to pay expenses," James Wellemeyer, June 2019, *marketwatch.com/story/even-with-a-hot-labor-market-one-third-of-americans-say-they-need-a-side-gig-to-pay-expenses-2019-06-07*

37. "2017 Allianz Generations Ahead Study," Allianz, May 2017, *allianzlife.com/-/media/files/global/documents/2017/09/21/18/00/2017-allianz-generations-ahead-fact-sheet.pdf*

38. "A Client's Perspective on Best Interest," WealthVest, Feb 2019, *wealthvest.com/wp-content/uploads/2019/02/12102-Best-Interest-White-Paper-Consumer-Facing.pdf*

39. "Average Annual Inflation Rates by Decade," Tim McMahon, 2019, *inflationdata.com/Inflation/Inflation/DecadeInflation.asp*

40. "Top Market Meltdowns over the Past 50 Years," Andrew DePietro, Dec 2017, *gobankingrates.com/investing/stocks/top-market-meltdowns/*

41. "Nerdwallet's 2019 Consumer Credit Card Report," Erin El Issa, Jul 2019, *nerdwallet.com/blog/credit-card-data/consumer-credit-card-trends-study/*

42. "2019 Survey Finds That Most People Believe Having a Will Is Important, but Less Than Half Have One," 2019, *caring.com/caregivers/estate-planning/wills-survey/*

43. "Why 85% of Americans Who Don't Have an FA Should," Alex Padalka, Nov 2018, *financialadvisoriq.com/c/2142463/253003*

44. "Here's the average 401(k) balance by age and how to raise yours," Adrian D. Garcia, May 2019, *bankrate.com/retirement/average-401k-balance-by-age/*

45. "The Average Salary by Age," Amelia Josephson, Apr 2019, *smartasset.com/retirement/the-average-salary-by-age*

46. "How long will my 401(k) savings last?," ShareBuilder Inc, 2019, *sharebuilder401k.com/help/401k-income*

47. "Investors Want Freedom With Retirement Savings," Lydia Saad, Jan 2018, *news.gallup.com/poll/225023/investors-no-strings-attached-retirement-income-stream.aspx*

48. Tom Mathews is a registered representative and investment advisor representative of Transamerica Financial Advisors, Inc. (TFA) and is an owner of How Money Works, LLC (HMW). HMW is separate from, and is not affiliated in any way with TFA. This book was written by Tom Mathews as an owner of HMW and not as a representative of TFA. This book was published by and is owned by HMW.

howmoneyworks.com 🔍

Visit our website.

Explore more resources to advance your
education and discover how you can
share financial literacy with all
the suckers you know and love.

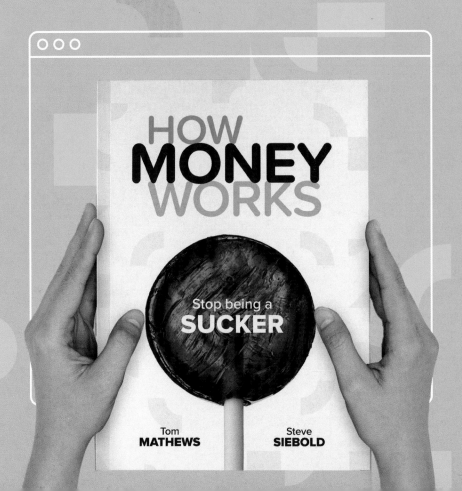